Alms for Oblivion

Alms for Oblivion

Poems by

William Heath

© 2024 William Heath. All rights reserved.
This material may not be reproduced in any form, published,
reprinted, recorded, performed, broadcast,
rewritten, or redistributed without
the explicit permission of William Heath.
All such actions are strictly prohibited by law.

Cover design by Shay Culligan
Cover photo by William Heath

ISBN: 978-1-63980-595-2

Kelsay Books
502 South 1040 East, A-119
American Fork, Utah 84003
Kelsaybooks.com

for Neal and Montse Learner
Good friends for many years

Acknowledgments

Thank you to the following publications, in which versions of these poems previously appeared or are forthcoming:

Adelaide Magazine: "At the Hop," "Of Hoops and Hopes," "The Scan," "St. Sebastian"
The Alembic: "Boccaccio's Theft," "A Bar in Santa Cruz" (an excerpt)
Avatar Review: "Cuban Story"
Baseball Bard: "The Rules of the Game"
Belt Magazine: "The Canfield Fair"
Beyond Words Literary Magazine: "Questions"
Cantos 2022: "Flyover Country," "At the Diner"
The Decadent Review: "On Poetry," "Just Beat It," "Trying to Say"
The Font: "The Lonely Side of the Lectern"
Glimpse: "Kentucky Cop"
Harbour Lights: "The Fall"
The High Window: "Blue Water House," "Mr. Beeghly's Doubts," "Bread," "Thick Milkshakes," "Ghosts"
Hurricane Review: "Circus Lore"
Indolent Books: a River Sings: "Alms for Oblivion"
In Parenthesis: "Sarah's House of Spirits," "Mirrors," "The New Wave" "Web of Deceit," "How Owls Kill," "The Myth of Flight," "Artists: Then & Now," "Fire," "Bats," "Losing It"
Last Leaves: "In Asturias"
Last Stanza Poetry Journal: "Masters Class"
Leaving Seville (a chapbook): "La Cueva de Pileta," "Artists: Then and Now"
LitBreak Magazine: "Night Nurse," reprinted in *A Plate of Pandemic*
Loch Raven Review: "The Future"
Misfit Magazine: "Remembering the Fifties"

Pennsylvania Literary Journal: "Chicago, 1968," "Bringing the War Home," "Fez"
Perceptions: "Forked Tongues"
Poetry Ireland: "Shaw in Russia"
Poetry Super Highway: "Old Guy"
Pulsebeat: "The Vet," "Dad's Last Days," "The Starlings of Rome"
Rye Whiskey River: "Key West Redux"
Sangam Literary Magazine: "John Wayne Stars As Sarge"
Schuylkill Valley Journal: "Neighbors"
Sequestrum: "Voluptuous Water"
Streetlight Magazine: "Purple Birds"
Tipton Poetry Journal: "Goalie"
Umbrella Factory Magazine: "At the Commune" "Ode to Alzheimer's," "Graduation Day," "The Ancients"
William & Mary Quarterly: "Don't Touch the Water"
Xavier Review: "The Curse of Rafinesque"

With thanks for their invaluable assistance and suggestions to Frank and Holly Bergon, Marty Malone, David Salner, and as always my beloved co-conspirator Roser Caminals-Heath

Contents

Part I   The Lonely Side of the Lectern

The Family Tree	19
Yardbird	21
Remembering the Fifties	22
Don't Touch the Water	23
The Canfield Fair	24
Mr. Beeghly's Doubts	25
At the Hop	27
Of Hoops and Hopes	28
Goalie	29
Le Gran Frappé	30
Questions	36
Chicago, 1968	37
Bringing the War Home	39
Shut It Down	40
The Vet	41
At the Commune	42
Voluptuous Water	43
Neighbors	44
Preacher Knox	46
Jail, No Bail	50
The Lonely Side of the Lectern	52
Graduation Day	53

Part II   Flyover Country

Flyover Country	57
At the Diner	58
A Diner in Tennessee	59
Boxcars	60
Bread	61

Sleep	62
White Noise	64
Alone with America	65
Las Vegas	66
Sarah's House of Spirits	67
The Curse of Rafinesque	69
Kentucky Cop	73
We get lost	74
Trunk Music	75
Circus Lore	76
The Rules of the Game	77
Sad Rally	78
How Democracy Fails	79

Part III Leaving Valin

Al Suelo	83
Chico a Chica	85
A Street Named Serpents	86
Galicia	87
In Asturias	88
La Cueva de la Pileta	89
Saint Sebastian	90
Mirrors	91
Leaving Valin	92
A Croatian Story	93
On the Rhine	95
Shaw in Russia	96
Fez	97
Barbados	98
Cuban Story	99

Part IV   The Starlings of Rome

The Starlings of Rome	103
The Rats of New York	105
Snake in the Lake	107
Nuku Hiva Bugs	108
Sunlight	109
How Owls Kill	110
Web of Deceit	111
Forked Tongues	112
Death in the Dunes	113
Elephants Have Long Noses	115
Good (and Bad) Vibrations	116
Bats	117
Losing It	118
A Zebra's Stripes	119
The Choice	120
On Leeches	121

Part V   Trying to Say

Alms for Oblivion	125
Boccaccio's Theft	126
The Myth of Flight	127
Masters Class	128
On Poetry	130
Just Beat It	132
Trying to Say	133
The Death of Lorca	134
Purple Birds	136
Artists: Then & Now	137

The New Wave	138
John Wayne Stars as Sarge	140
Count Dracula	141

Part VI   Waiting for the End

Waiting for the End	145
Night Nurse	147
Posthumous Poems	149
The Scan	150
Blue Water House	151
Jimmy Buffet	153
Key West Redux	154
Nobody's Home	155
On Memory and Forgetting	156
The Ancients	158
The Invention of Love	159
Ghosts	160
The Digital Age	162
Old Guy	163
Ode to Alzheimer's	164
The Fall	165
Thick Milkshakes	167
Dad's Last Days	168
The Future	169

Time hath, my lord,
A wallet at his back, wherein he puts
Alms for oblivion, a great-sized monster
Of ingratitudes. Those scraps are good deeds past,
Which are devoured as fast as they are made,
Forgot as soon as done. Perseverance, dear my lord,
Keeps honor bright. To have done is to hang
Quite out of fashion . . .
—*Troilus and Cressida*

Part I

The Lonely Side of the Lectern

The Family Tree

1

In 1817 Edward Heath comes to Ohio,
a man of fine education (his mother
taught in Tyringham, Mass.), called
Capt. Heath, he surveys townships
into sections, the work being carefully
and accurately done, lives in Hardscrabble,
later Maryville in Medina County.
We keep his muzzle-loader and
powder horn above our mantle.

2

Albert Gallatin Heath, a mere boy,
shoots the largest deer ever killed
in the county during the 1800s.
Known as "the Big Buck," this deer
has been the object of the hunt for
every able-bodied man in the area.
One day young Albert, who later
becomes an avid hunter and trapper,
is in the woods when he hears a shot;
soon the big deer, still untouched,
comes crashing out of the thicket
toward him. One shot brings
the proud beauty down. That buck
dresses out at 254 pounds, his antlers
are fashioned into knife handles.
Many years later these knives
are still used in the Heath family.
At ninety-one he passes away after
scything in Myrtle Hill Cemetery.

3

Albert R. Heath is a meat cutter
in the kitchen of the insane asylum
in Newburg, near Cleveland. My
great grandfather Heath remembers
playing along the outside fence
where some of the inmates
toss watermelons to children
who often gather there.

Yardbird

A hyper-active boy bent on
exploring the neighborhood.
To curb my wanderlust, Mom
devises a harness with a rope
attached to the clothesline
in the backyard stretching

from apple to pear tree.
Constrained by this device
I still have considerable
leeway to mosey about.
Picture me in a sunsuit,
strapped in a halter

fastened to a clothesline
so that I can putter at will
on the grass—while Mom
stands at the kitchen sink,
sudsy dishrag in her hand,
keeping watch at the window.

Remembering the Fifties

There are five of us in all:
Ozzie, Harriet, me, sis, our dog Spot.
A dutiful wifey with a favorite charity
and a pure devotion to hubby's ambitions,
Mom is homemaker, Dad breadwinner,
their dream is to live happily ever after
somewhere in suburbia. A woman's role
is to provide an emotional outlet for
her man, a comfy hearth where he can
gird his loins for another day of fierce
struggle in the marketplace. Dad
tells Mom that his production goal
for her is two boys, two girls.

Men want women who will bolster
their egos, flip their eggs, and make
their beds. Girls take cooking, date
appeal, marriage, personal etiquette.
Boys study carpentry, auto mechanics,
metalwork. Sis gets an A in home econ,
I flunk shop. At college she majors
in marriage. In those days Italian women
set the tone with their big breasts and
emotional outbursts. In swirl dress
with Singer vacuum, Mom, the happy
housewife, does her chores until the day
Dad runs off with his secretary.

Don't Touch the Water

In 1951, when I am nine,
our town's Little League loses
to a team from Youngstown
that wins the city championship.

To celebrate they all go to
the municipal pool for a picnic.
The lifeguard will not let
Al Bright, the only Black player,

in the water. Instead, he stays
outside the fence and watches
everyone else diving off
the high board and swimming.

One of his teammates
brings a Coke and hotdog,
some sit with him waiting
for the rest to clear the area.

Finally, the lifeguard provides
an inflated raft and pushes him
one time around the pool:
"Don't you dare touch the water."

The Canfield Fair

for Joel Beeghly

A carnival odor of cooking oil
poured over roasting peanuts,
a squinting man taking aim
at a file of white ducks
sliding along a conveyor belt.

The boys loading sheep
onto a pickup keep
one hand under the throat
while the other has a grip
on the tail and asshole.

The smell of moldy straw
and cow dung in the air
reminds me of playing hide-
and-seek in the hayloft
of my grandfather's barn.

We stay up all night sampling
the home-baked cherry pies
the ladies of the Methodist Church
expect us to stay up all night
to protect, while dreaming

of ponytailed baton twirlers,
lithe legs beneath short skirts
that reveal pink panties when
they prance down the midway
tossing batons at the sky.

Mr. Beeghly's Doubts

Mr. Beeghly has his doubts
whether I am a suitable playmate
for his son and my friend Joel.
He calls me a Johnny Come Lately
and a Fly By Nighter, although I
only break into their house once
to retrieve a basketball.
                          It isn't
hard: I ascend the television pole
on the side of the house near
an open second-story window,
then it's down the stairs,
through living room and kitchen
to the garage where the pebbly
surfaced sphere of my desire
is waiting for me.
                          You see
they have the best backboard
and rim in the neighborhood
fastened to their two-car garage.
I am guilty, I know, but feel
completely innocent. Isn't
basketball my avocation, don't I
answer its call every day?

And yes I am known to rob
their orchard of apples, plums,
and pears when I'm hungry,
to pick grapes from their arbor,
and ride Joel's pony, but only
with his permission.

                    And yes
I teach Joel to swing out on
tree vines before splashing
into Lee Run Creek in spite of
repeated warnings the water
is shallow, we could break
a leg or our necks on the rocks.
After Mr. Beeghly chops off
the offending vines, we simply
seek others further downstream.

At the Hop

After the game there is always
a sock hop in the gym: we dance
the stroll, the funky slop, the jitterbug,
the bunny hop, and still find time

to twist and shout. Bill Halley, a kiss
curl on his forehead, starts us all
rocking around the clock, girls wet
their panties screaming at a fat man,

weighed down by diamonds, who
finds his thrill on Blueberry Hill,
the Everly Brothers sing "Wake up,
Little Susie," Ricky Nelson of the

dreamy bedroom eyes, Little Richard
of the foot-high flattop, Jerry Lee Lewis
mangles his piano, pretty boy Frankie
Avalon in suit and tie asks Venus

to enter his lonely life, but most of all
Elvis of the swivel hips and kiss-me lips,
puts down his friends as hound dogs
while making the jailhouse rock,

and we all cry when Buddy Holly and
the Big Bopper perish in a plane crash.
Yet, contra Don McLean's "American Pie,"
to this day the music never dies.

Of Hoops and Hopes

My Dad once told me I had
the best jump shot he ever saw,
a testimony to how few games
he'd been to yet a touching tribute
any son would treasure.

Back before the three-point line,
I had a smooth long-distance stroke,
not only on my jump shot but also
a one-hand set shot, another one-hand shot
that resembled the motion of a layup,

and a two-hand set shot I learned
at Dolph Shayes's basketball camp.
By the time the three-point line arrived
my hops were gone along with
what might-have-been.

Goalie

I crouch on my toes
before the goal knowing
how quickly a kicked ball
can humiliate ten useless
sausages I call my fingers
and the dinosaurian pace
a message reaches the brain.

The enemy throw triumphant
hands in the air, hug each other
as if the war were over,
while I turn to retrieve
the white sphere that lies
behind me on the ground
at the back of the net
as docile as a skull.

Le Gran Frappé

for Marshall Dunn

Watch the ball, bend your knees,
a hundred dollars please.
                —The tennis pro's song

1

I've known the pleasure of dancing
to the cadences of swatting a felt ball
back and forth across a low net
with movements marked by
elegance and grace.

Yet there are levels to the game.
One summer with other college players
I am a counselor at a ritzy tennis camp
in the Adirondacks, play a set with
the resident pro Joe Fishback.

He's faced the greats of his era
and naturally he beats me six-o.
On one point I recall smashing three
consecutive overheads to opposite sides
of the court, yet Joe is waiting there

in perfect position for his return until
my fourth smash sails outside the lines.
He can tell by the way I run back
for the lob, how I leap and twist,
where my shot will land.

Of Joe's two sons, Pete is nationally
ranked in his age group; Mike, barely
taller than the net, possesses a full
repertoire of shots. After years of
skilled training both will turn pro.

2

I didn't play competitive matches
until my sophomore year at Hiram.
My roommate Gary Marks, a very
good player, urges me to try out,
we become doubles partners.

I am a talented all-around athlete
but I'd never had a tennis lesson
in my life. Thanks to quick reflexes
I can poach at the net, my other shots
are amateurish and erratic.

This is back in the days when
all tennis balls are white, as are
the players, except for the great
Arthur Ashe, and all rackets are
made of lovely laminated wood.

Gary is a fierce competitor—once,
after a bad call, he crosses to his
opponent's side, is told, "Game's not
over," and Gary replies, "Just checking
to see if the lines are still here."

"When in doubt call it out,"
is the cynical advice players are
given nowadays, thus inserting
a fundamental dishonesty into
a once honorable game.

3

From my summer tennis camp
I learn how the game is played, spending
long days in the sun to work on my
serve, overhead, ground strokes,
footwork, stamina, strategy.

Tennis is chess with pieces
that won't stay put. You must think
on the run about pace, placement,
while the ball bounces toward you
at various spins, speeds, angles.

By my ripe age, however, I have
too many bad habits to ever excel.
I coach a college team in Lexington,
at local tournaments I win some gilded
Tennis Man Serving trophies.

I become good enough to smack
once in a while the kind of shots
the pros hit on every point, that only
keeps me competitive with players
like my friend Marshall Dunn.

Teammates at Hiram, we still
play together after sixty years.
Roughly speaking, I am victorious
for some thirty years, while he
dominates the last decades.

My best shot is an inside-out forehand
cracking winners at obtuse angles
aimed to elude an opponent's racket;
but Marshall has a strong backhand
so if I miss my target I'm dead.

The drop shot, a wounded dove
that flutters over the cord and falls
very close to the net is another of
his wicked tricks, out of reach of
anyone not named Rafael Nadal.

We both try to hit deep, knowing
the mantra is to punish the short ball,
if a cripple comes your way kill it,
save your courtesy for the post-
match-point handshake at the net.

Now our knees are shot (rotator
cuff torn, tennis elbow strained),
just two old guys standing in place
to swat brisk balls back to where
they're easiest to get.

After an hour of such strokes
we look forward to lunch.

4

I save my serve for last. When I am
young it is my signature. Serve and charge
the net to hit a short volley with a compact
swing, like a carpenter driving a nail, is,
if I reach the return, my game.

A hard-hit serve turns a tennis ball
oval in the air, intense spin creates
a fuzzy blur, the astonishing speed
hard to capture on television, is clear
if you're standing beside the court.

It seems impossible to compete against
such speed and power, yet step into
that cosmos, enter the aura of the game,
and the body instinctively adjusts,
you are, as they say, in the zone.

For my serve I toe the line, left hand
bounces the ball an occult number
of times, three is good, so is seven,
then toss the ball skyward, not,
if possible, in the sun, coil back

by bending my knees and reaching
behind me with the racket as if
to scratch my spine, and at the exact
moment when it seems the ball is
suspended a split second in a pillow

of air at the apex of the toss I
spring forward and strike it with
the tensile strength of my magic
graphite whip as a resounding
whack echoes across the court.

What gives power to my serve is
how high I leap to hit a smash
similar to my hardest overheads.
No foot fault can be called since
my feet are too far above the court.

Only rarely did I accomplish this feat.
My normal serve is nothing to fear,
yet the apotheosis of my tennis career
comes at a public court in Montreal
when my serve is at its very best.

A crowd gathers and calls for others
to come see *"le gran frappé."*

Questions

After the movie I ask her
what song the sirens sang,
which name Achilles assumed
hiding among the women,
whether lost love, like old bones,
calcifies, ossifies, or turns to stone.

Why, if you stand in the dark,
can you see someone in the light,
but not vice versa? How is it
a voice is audible through a wall?
If I listen, am I present, and how
can I verify this? Do you think being
is round? If so, where should it go?

How do you conceive of the cosmos?
Have you spoken with God and does
His or Her voice have an accent?
Did He or She have a form?

Should a king, in her opinion,
go to the sacred grove and kill
his old predecessor? Why do we
fear dead bodies? Have you
listened to the flowers
wearing out their colors?

It was our first and last date.

Chicago, 1968

The Youth International Party—Yippies—
bring Pigasus, a 125-pound hog they
nominate for President. At curfew time
cops swinging nightsticks charge Lincoln Park,
drive the crowd down North Side streets.

On Tuesday by a ten-foot cross we sing
"We Shall Overcome," then 300 cops
wade in using tear gas—we throw bottles,
stones, tip over park benches, improvise
barricades. Next Mayor Daley refuses

permission for a march from Grant Park
to the amphitheater. A "police riot"
forces us onto Michigan Avenue. Cops
in visored helmets meet us at the Hilton,
headquarters for Humphrey, McCarthy.

Television cameras broadcast shocking
images of social chaos live to the nation.
The police attack in two flying wedges,
drag protestors to paddy wagons,
battering many. My mantra "Dump

the Hump" as two of Chicago's finest
toss me through a Haymarket Lounge
picture window, flying shards cut
my scalp, bloody some customers
(in a recurring dream I land on a table

in a French restaurant between
the vichyssoise and fricandeau.)
The Hilton's air conditioning
sucks in tear gas, spreads it
to each room. McCarthy kids

on the fifteenth floor pelt cops with
whatever objects are at hand. The police
storm the hotel, club anybody in reach.
We chant "the whole world is watching,"
89 million Americans are.

Bringing the War Home

Weathermen view Panthers as vanguard
of the anti-imperialist struggle.
Weather communes smash monogamy,
favor group gropes, criticism sessions
to purge the last vestiges of individuality.
"Nothing comes before the collective,"
pointing to a mattress on the floor.

Days of Rage proclaim revolution
by the deed: trash Chicago's Gold Coast,
kick ass, break glass of the ruling class,
show some guts, bring the war home.
Everyone chants "Ho, Ho, Ho Chi Minh,
The NLF is gonna win" and "Hey, hey, LBJ,
how many kids did you kill today?"

Yippies plaster See Canada Now
posters on the Army Recruiting Center,
shoot water pistols, throw meringue pies
at tuxedoed notables, dress like witches
to levitate the Pentagon, toss dollars
off the balcony of the Stock Exchange.
No pay toilets ("Let my people go")
a key revolutionary demand, a Festival
of Life held in Lincoln Park adjacent
to Old Town where the tribes gather.

Back at the pad Yippies come and go,
rapping of chairmen Mao and Ho,
storm the Pentagon, dreaming of Che,
while grunts dreaming of Sgt. York
hump the boonies in search of
little yellow men in black pajamas
and hope they don't buy the farm.

Shut It Down

I hunch up in a windowsill trying
to see speakers at the podium through
the pot smoke. We fear if we don't
shut the place down it will revert

to repressive tactics of having
homecomings, seminars on the lawn.
Teachers who attend their classes
are scabs, fierce scuffles break out

in the halls, professorial pipes spill,
notes scatter. Political panty raids
follow: trash cans set ablaze,
paint-filled balloons thrown at bourgeois,

library window glass shatters,
slogans chanted, fists raised, fire alarms
set off, the swimming pool liberated,
the administration building stormed

to take the dean hostage, but it's
Friday and nobody's around.
No classes today, we theorize,
means no ruling class tomorrow.

The Vet

At a gas station the smell
of diesel fuel, at a construction site
it is wet clay that brings him
back to Vietnam, when driving
he keeps a nervous eye at any
tree line along the road. For years
he dreads the 4th of July.
Walking in the woods he is wary
of pongee sticks and snipers.

When they tell him he goes
upstairs and shaves his head.
He'd done a tour in the Mekong,
been exposed to Agent Orange.
He believes in rebirth not God,
between chemo sessions he lights
a joss stick, tosses the I Ching,
listens to the Rolling Stones.
Three months later he dies.

At the Commune

At Better Living Through
Chemistry, aka Maggie's Farm,
I put a tab under my tongue,
wait for the world to change:
everybody tokes then talks
without exhaling as if
their strained voices were
rehearsing death-bed speeches.

The women bake bread,
brown rice and beans
a typical meal, barefoot kids
named Lucy in the Sky
with Diamonds, Rosemary,
Thyme, Ruby Tuesday,
and Give Peace a Chance,
sport Day-Glo painted faces.

The plan is if women stop
shaving their legs men will
treat them as equals, not
merely as sex objects.—
more or less this works.

They dance naked around
a maypole, wood flutes
and dulcimers. Everyone
into cleaning their karma,
not washing the dishes.

In the lotus position all day
he chants a Veda mantra.
A joss stick burning
by the waterbed, she likes
fucking to otherworldly
sounds of singing whales.

Voluptuous Water

In a stone house in a forest
near Woodstock money might
flow my way if I can provide
an alternative to the chemical

cocktail piped by the public
system. My plan to cash in:
a bottled-water business,
selling two brands: Wild Water
for normal use, Voluptuous Water
for those special occasions—

same brew, different price—
both drawn from a deep cistern
dug by a family from Italy,
a land of ancient aqueducts,
who built my lovely home.

Years later bottled water
becomes a fad in yuppie circles,
serious money is made.
The water from my well, I swear,
was exceptional, the best I've

ever savored, mineral content
high and healthy, the drink
refreshing, worth paying for.
I don't regret not turning a profit
but I do miss that pure taste.

Neighbors

The guy with the Walt Whitman beard
lives down the valley in a clapboard
colonial house so close to the road
you can judge its age. One evening
he shows up at my front door, wants
to talk. I have only a few neighbors
yet I don't ask him in.

As we stand on my fieldstone porch
I note his bicycle tipped on its side,
wire handlebar basket brimming over
with quart bottles of cheap beer.
I often see him pedaling into town
two miles away to replenish his stash.
His ruby face betrays he's far gone
before he spills his slurred words.

NASA has rejected three-hundred-
and-sixty-seven of his inventions because
it has been taken over by Venusians
from outer space. I nod and ask how
he knows who they are. They have
a strange look about them, their heads
aren't on straight.

Weeks later, wandering in woods
that frame this valley located between
Esopus and New Paltz, close to
the Hudson River, I come upon him
crouched by a small waterfall
rearranging stones, he looks up
and says, "I think Nature should look
as neat as possible, don't you?"

Each weekend his gentleness is belied
when his mother brings food and clothes,
hauls off the laundry. Their fierce arguments
last hours, horrific screams echo
in the valley. I fear he'll strangle her,
yet the following day he's out puttering in
his yard, the next Sunday his mother
drives up with fresh supplies.

Preacher Knox

1

There is something compelling
about a man named Moses
walking into a town named Liberty
in Mississippi's Amite county
(friendship, in French) where
no Black person is free.

That's what Bob Moses does in 1961,
working to register Black voters.
In late August he leads local farmers,
Curtis Dawson and Alfred Knox,
down to the courthouse to fill out
a daunting registration form.

Suddenly two white men attack,
one hits Moses repeatedly in the temple
with the blunt end of a switch-blade,
knocking him to the sidewalk where
he curls up to protect his head.
Knox, a part-time preacher, tries

to pull Bob's assailant away while
Dawson pleads with the man to stop.
Moses has an out-of-body experience,
as if he were floating off the ground
and looking down at himself before
coming to, T-shirt drenched in blood.

Knox urges him to leave the scene,
but Moses insists on pressing charges,
entering the courthouse only to learn
that Billy Jack Caston, his attacker,
is the sheriff's cousin. Against
all odds, Moses files charges.

Back in McComb, Dr. James Anderson
needs nine stiches to sew Bob's scalp,
wraps bandages around the wound.
Moses returns to Liberty the next day
for the hearing, a courtroom filled
with white men brandishing shotguns.

Caston claims Moses, crouching
like a kung fu master, attacked him.
The sheriff says it's too dangerous for Bob
to tell his side of the story. He, Knox,
and Dawson are hurried out a back door,
the judge finds Billy Jack innocent.

2

Thirty years later I drive into Liberty
to research what happened there
during the Civil Rights movement.
Herbert Lee had been killed at a local
cotton gin, Louis Allen, a witness,
was gunned down in his driveway.

Moses and his fellow SNCC workers
leave the area in 1961; Preacher Knox,
a local farmer, stands his ground,
still lives outside Liberty.
I give him a call, ask if I can come
to his home to tape an interview.

I follow his directions through
a maze of backcountry dirt roads,
no street signs, no names on mailboxes,
eventually I pull up at his house,
a weatherboard cabin with tin roof,
stone chimney, small front porch.

Knox is one of a few Blacks in Liberty
who, thanks to a New Deal program,
buys forty acres of land in 1939,
thus fulfilling a Reconstruction promise
some seventy years too late. We sit on
a bench supported by two large trees.

I remember how the hens cluck
and peck at the front yard dirt.
I place a recorder between us
and as we talk chickens strut
beneath the bench, still clucking.
A rooster voices his opinion.

A large-framed man wearing blue
denim overalls, a chambray shirt,
Knox explains how hard it is
to be a small farmer: "Ain't nothin'
folks can do 'cept scratch it out in
the summer, strap it in the winter."

When I ask about Moses and Liberty,
Knox calls to his grandson, elbow deep
in a tractor engine: "Come here, Henry,
I don't think you've heard this story."
A sullen well-built teenager strolls
over to us, reluctantly.

As Knox relates in detail
what happened the day he goes
to the Liberty courthouse to "redish,"
the boy's face changes to respect.
He didn't know his grandfather
is a hero, stood up to the Man.

As we are conversing I notice
pickups cruising by more
frequently than you'd expect on
a back country road. Are they
other farmers or has word spread
about a white man asking questions?

The statute of limitations does not
expire in murder cases. Before I go
I ask him who shot Louis Allen.
He shares my suspicion of the sheriff.
Driving away, I see a grandfather
talking with his grandson.

Jail, No Bail

for SNCC

At Parchman we're stripped
and searched, issued a towel,
a bar of soap, a toothbrush,
sheets and pillow cases,
a striped prison outfit.
Filthy cells full of bugs.

A jail is just another house,
less comfortable than most,
I admit, room service leaves
something to be desired,
if you like three squares
of rice and beans you can't

complain, a mattress thick
as a poor man's wallet
and twice as hard, no seat
on the toilet, rusty water
seeps from the tap, a view
through iron bars of a guy

in another cell staring back.
One visitor asked us to say
something in "commonist."
Entertainment is not out
of the question, cigarettes
smoked down to the filter

serve as chess pieces,
singing freedom songs
always lifts our spirits,
drives the guards crazy.
They take our sheets,
then our mattresses,

and, when we refuse to
keep quiet, our soap,
towels, and toothbrushes,
yet we don't stop singing,
"Keep your eyes on
the prize, hold on."

The Lonely Side of the Lectern

Any good teacher has an ideal
of the perfect professor who teaches
anyone and inspires everyone
to want to learn, so when you walk

into a class and all you see are
droopy eyes and folded arms
you tend to blame yourself.
You want to bring them to life,

give them some of your own blood
if necessary, but what's the point
of donating blood to vegetables?
You come to resent your students

as some doctors hate the terminally
ill who make them feel inadequate
by refusing to respond to treatment.
I'd rather teach the mentally

challenged, formerly known as
retarded people, who try more
than these zombies wasting my
time and their parents' money.

Graduation Day

Each year I look forward
to graduation day, the coeds
wash their hair, let it flow
freely to their shoulders,

somehow long black gowns
only showing their ankles are
alluring, the press of breasts
against thin cloth, the carefully

made-up faces suggest a
bounteous world of beauty.
It is always spring then,
a time to put blooming life

on display, the world is all
before them, and I wish
them well, even though I know
brightness falls from the air.

Part II

Flyover Country

Flyover Country

We in the Midwest are
dismissed as flyover country
seen through the scratched
acrylic of an airplane window.

An elevated position implies
power—yet what do people
in the air know about what's
happening on the ground?

We folks down below look up
and out, we see the plane
skimming over us with disdain.
Beware of our resentment.

At the Diner

The waitress with a glass eye
winks at me, calls me hon,
serves up a slice of cherry pie
as big as the plate
                      One look
at her face and I know waiting
tables at a roadside restaurant
isn't where she wants to be
by this time in her life.
                      How
she got here probably had
something to do with a man
not being the kind of guy
he was supposed to be.
                      Now
truck drivers tickle her palm
when they tip, offer to take her
anywhere her heart desires.

A Diner in Tennessee

The waitress's white uniform
is sprinkled with green spots,
a dark gout of ketchup stains
her right hip. She scowls and asks
what I want in the kind of voice
someone certain she is dying
and deeply bitter about it might
ask her doctor, "What have I got?"

Truck drivers stack elbows
on the counter, drink black coffee
from thick-lipped white mugs,
talk straight to a skinny waitress
while a slow fan chases its tail
and buzzing flies try to brain
themselves on the screen door.

Abandoned gas pumps out front
date from when regular was fifty-
seven cents a gallon. Hines
Root Beer sign riddled with
rusted-out bullet holes. Large letters
on the barn roof across the road
SEE ROCK CITY.

Boxcars

I hear a relentless
mechanical rumble,
red eyes wink at me
in the night as a long line

of rusty yellow boxcars
begin their redundant
chain dance, screeching
across my rusty nerves

on steel wheels like a bad
dream that will not quit,
followed by a series of
flatbed cars heaped with

twisted metal, scrap iron,
until at last comes a blue
caboose pulling its sweet
cargo of silence.

Bread

The best thing in
the world to break
is bread, wheat fresh
from the fields, fire
preferably of wood,
squeeze the dough
in your fingers until
it forms a shapely
lump, place it in
a heated iron oven
and watch it swell
in a sudden pregnancy
and within an hour
emerge as a plump
baby, complete if
you look closely for
a navel of sorts
and a golden skin
with a crisp crunch
outside, a warm treat for
the tongue inside plus
a lingering aftertaste—
this is the gift of bread.

Sleep

Though this visible world seems formed in love,
the invisible spheres were formed in fright.
　　　　　　　　　　　　—Melville

Sleep is a greater mystery
than we want to admit,
we know it restores
us for the coming day,
shutting the body down
in order to start back up
again in the morning,
yet that's not an adequate

explanation of the process
by which we die and live
so many times. We know
dreams often help us
to stay asleep. They
play variations, Freud says,
on our unconscious or
conscious concerns of

the previous day,
but not all, I'd even
say most, dreams fit
that formula. They are
far more puzzling,
have no clear connection
to our waking selves.
Nightmares the most

elusive mystery of all.
Sometimes they startle us
awake in a cold sweat
in sheer fright. What's
so natural about that,
what purpose is served?
Or is fright the message
of our darkest nights?

White Noise

What Pythagoras calls
the music of the spheres,
those celestial sounds
from the seven planets,
is drowned out by what
we say is white noise,
a constant hum we're now
accustomed to, like the
ringing in my ears I do
my best not to hear.

It comes from highways,
all that rubber meeting
the road, all those engines
guzzling fossil fuel.
Just as the haze of
air pollution hides
the Milky Way, a truly
awesome sight, so
this steady noise we
try to ignore simply
diminishes us.

Alone with America

Every car commercial on TV
features its product kicking up dust
as it veers off the paved road
to violate a wilderness area,
causing irreparable harm
to one ecosystem or another.

                        That's
what sells: manly men and risk-
taking empowered women
venturing into uncharted territory
to play at being pioneers off
the beaten track, charge up
mountains, from vertiginous peaks
gaze out at the setting sun.

Cars are not for commuting,
picking up groceries, taking kids
to soccer games, driving safely
on highways. It's the alone
with America fantasy, free
to do what the heart desires,
no restrictions, no consequences.

We can be anything we want to be,
who cares whose fragile habitat
our radial tires destroy, we are
the world, we are the children.

Las Vegas

In our age of global warming
America's fastest growing city
sits in the midst of a desert.
Las Vegas is American reality
with rough edges rubbed off.

It is a mirage you come to
for affirmation not challenge,
a place where you lose
far more than the money
you put in gaming machines.

The basic Las Vegas strategy
is to make average folks
feel special while they are
being ripped off just like
everybody else. Residents

proudly proclaim the city
is the Twenty-First Century
unfolding before our eyes
in all its ersatz high-rise glory,
while with set smiles those

feeding evaporating dollars
into insatiable machines
that enrich a few fat cats
keep insisting they feel
happy, happy, happy.

Sarah's House of Spirits

Sarah Winchester marries the son
of the man who invents the Winchester
repeater, the Gun that Won the West,
a medium tells her that unless she builds
more rooms to her house to host and
appease the spirits of thousands killed
by the notorious rifle, she will die—
so for thirty-eight years she adds room
after room, door after door, endless corridors,
stained glass spider-web windows, twisted
stairways, parquet floors of mahogany,
teak, ash, oak, and other choice woods,
silver-plated chandeliers, secret
passages to elude pursuing ghosts.

Each night she visits the Séance Room
to learn what next needs to be done.
This calls for continual renovation
as the house expands to five-hundred
rooms, shrinks to one-hundred-and-sixty.
The resulting maze has an upside down
column that doesn't touch the ceiling,
chimneys that never reach the roof.
Windows in the Grand Ballroom feature
obscure Shakespeare quotes: "Wide
unclasp the tables of their thoughts,"
"These same thoughts people this
little world." Gnomic messages inciting
her obsessions? No one knows.

The San Francisco earthquake of 1906
severely damages the house, Sarah
is rescued from her wrecked bedroom,
she sees the quake as a sign to change
her ways, thirty front rooms are sealed.
An eight-story tower falls, other turrets,
towers, cupolas, and balconies remain.
The number thirteen figures prominently
in her extravagant designs. Thirteen
the number of window panes, ceiling panels,
stairway steps. Among flowers, fountains,
statues, and exotic trees highlighting
her resplendent gardens, thirteen palm trees
lining the driveway die of old age.

The Curse of Rafinesque

Make it new
—Ezra Pound

Constantinus Rafinesque, born near Istanbul,
as a young man leaves Palermo for Philadelphia.
Short, corpulent, with an outsized head,
thin refined hands, dark penetrating eyes,
tangled black hair to his shoulders—he is
convinced the Americas abound with new
species that he will discover and name.

Part idiot savant, part autodidact,
Rafinesque is hired by Horace Holley,
president of Transylvania, to teach
natural history, botany, foreign languages.
Named for an early Kentucky land company,
under Holley the college's reputation rises,
draws many students from the Old South.

Holley's wife Sarah takes a special interest
in Rafinesque, whose slovenly appearance
cries out for a mother's care. She feeds him,
washes his clothes, struggles to comb
his unruly hair. At the Holleys's frequent
parties, when not moping in a corner,
Rafinesque enthralls with tales of botanizing.

Hardships are formidable: gnats dance
before his eyes, ticks stick to his skin,
ants crawl his ears, mosquitoes bite,
wasps sting, knee-deep in swamp mud,
dangers of poisonous snakes, trees
toppling in thunderstorms, flash floods,
a black bear attacks in a canebrake.

Yet he loves to explore this new world:
clear skies, a bracing breeze, breathing
pure country air, a draught of cool water
from the brook. Each species he names
a small conquest over Nature's bounty.
He feels religious wandering in God's
wide temple not made by hands.

To some he is the best field botanist
of his time, collecting specimens of fish,
snakes, lizards, frogs, bats, insects,
and plants that he swears are unique.
To others he is absolutely delusional,
many of his so-called discoveries bogus,
claims extravagant, findings trash.

Audubon recalls how Rafinesque arrives
at his door in a long yellow coat stained
with plant juice, huge pockets stuffed
with specimens he insists are not merely
new species, but a new genus. That night
his naked guest smashes his best violin
swatting an open-window invasion of bats.

Rafinesque is fascinated by aboriginal
peoples of the Americas, he collects
vocabularies, copies Maya glyphs,
argues that a comparative study
of languages will reveal where the Indians
come from, when and how they migrate
and disperse across two continents.

Once again his passion for novelty
creates controversy. His translation
from the original tablets (now lost)
of the *Wolum Olum,* the Delaware text
of their sacred origin legend, creation
and flood myths, is accepted for years
before declared an elaborate hoax.

A few years earlier the Angel Moroni
gives Joseph Smith—from golden plates
(now lost)—a translation of a sacred epic,
The Book of Mormon. Yet Rafinesque
does anticipate later language studies,
his two-volume work on Native American
use of medicinal plants now invaluable.

Thanks to President Holley, Transylvania
becomes a college where reason is favored
over revelation, students are trained
to lead good, useful, happy lives.
These liberal positions are anathema,
orthodox protestant clergy fear Holley
esteems Socrates over Jesus.

A nasty rumor to discredit Holley
suggests Rafinesque is having an affair
with his wife, causes the offended botanist
to leave in 1826, putting his curse on Holley,
the college, consigning them to divine justice.
Holley resigns the next year, dies shortly
afterwards of yellow fever.

In 1828 Old Morrison—Gideon's Shryock's
celebrated Greek Revival building, the heart
of the Transylvania campus, its pediment
supported by six strong Doric columns—
burns to the ground. Rafinesque credits
his curse, predicts *I might yet live to see
my mature insanity become wisdom.*

When Rafinesque dies in Philadelphia,
the landlord refuses to release the body,
planning to sell it to recoup back rent,
his friends lower the corpse by ropes
out a window, bury it in a cemetery.
Years later the college moves the remains
to a crypt under Old Morrison.

Rafinesque's curse lives on: Old Morrison
burns down two more times. In 1961
college coed Betty Gail Brown is strangled
with her own bra in a car parked a few
yards from Rafinesque's tomb. In spite
of multiple confessions, no conviction,
her murder still unsolved.

Kentucky Cop

In the real world I know a cop
who got in his car to chase a crook
through the streets of Lexington.

You've seen this scene in movies:
siren whines, tires screech and smoke,
shots fired, but the cop loses

control of his car—pavement
slick, he doesn't have rack-
and-pinion steering, he's no

stunt driver, there are potholes—
so he swerves into a skid, the car
comes up on the sidewalk, hits

an old lady killing her instantly,
injuring several bystanders.
The crook never caught. The cop

takes to drink, fights with his wife
over quitting the force. She throws
a punch, breaks his nose. It never

heals properly. He loves his wife;
he's also afraid of her. She sleeps
around, dares him to do something

about it. He sips bonded bourbon,
watches TV, talks to himself.
A sweet guy who cries easily.

We get lost

on our way to the Capitol Hill Cinema
where *Prince of the City* is playing.
I stop for directions at a liquor store
in a small roadside shopping mall.
Two Black men in red jackets behind
the counter can't agree on how
to go. A guy in a tattered army jacket

with bulging pockets in the doorway,
a can of beer pressed to his cheek,
says follow him. Assuming he has a car
we go outside, instead he walks over
to ours and without thinking I let him
in the back seat. Before I can exit
one red-jacketed man from the store

knocks on the window, "Keep calm,
I'm a cop," he growls. "Get out of
that man's car." The guy in back
whines in protest," Oh, man, what
you doin? I'm tryin to help this dude,
don't give me no hard time. I'll
remember this one, baby. You're

in my book now." "That's alright
with me. Just get your ass outa here,"
the cop says with a scowl, then
turns to me: "You don't want
to let yourself get set up like that,
not around here." "I thought he
had a car," I explain. "So did he,"

the cop says laughing, "So did he."

Trunk Music

for Bob Leuci

Vinny Albano is shot
six times in the chest
by a wiseguy for sleeping
with his ex-wife.

On his death bed
the DA begs for
his assailant's name.
Vinny refuses, survives.

On a cop's salary he owns
a liquor store, a candy shop,
a house on the ocean,
plus apartment buildings,

a condo in Florida, a yacht.
The next time, lights out.
His pink slip an ice pick
to the nape of the neck.

His body is rolled
in a carpet, stuffed
in a car trunk, left at
an airport parking lot.

Circus Lore

Lion tamer in
gold lamé tights,
his silver shirt of silk
open to the waist.

His gypsy wife worries
most when he's back
stage taking chances
with the showgirls
who hug the midget,

tell him he's cute—
while he cops a feel,
kisses their breasts—
get all huffy when
he says what else
he'd like to do.

The midget hates kids.
They laugh, point,
call him silly names,
try rough stuff.
Ditto for the acrobat
with gold-capped teeth

whose worst nightmare
is of one false step
some Saturday morning,
a lethal fall before
a half-full house of kids
drooling popcorn.

The Rules of the Game

A case can be made that baseball's
best play is a foul ball into the stands,
a lucky fan gets a souvenir, the batter
another swing, the pitcher one more
chance for an out. A win-win situation
all around, especially if you don't
know the rules of the game that from
this perspective are arbitrary.

On the other hand, a devoted fan
rooting for players on a particular team
doesn't cheer for foul balls. If you side
with the batter you feel badly he didn't
get a hit, if the pitcher, no strikeout,
ground out, or easy fly. A foul ball
is merely the status quo, the chance
for victory or defeat hasn't budged.

Sad Rally

Trump is the trumpet,
the avenger for folks
who get to get even
as he puts coastal elites
down, mocks and scorns
those who oppose
his vain whims.

He calls them scum,
sad losers his favorite
words, and secretly
all you sad losers
in red MAGA caps
shouting at his rallies
must sigh with relief

he's not picking on you
but your enemies,
all those fortunate ones
who caught the breaks
you missed out on,
and those dark others
enjoying the benefits

that you deserved
who should be sent back
where they came from.
You who feel left out,
ignored, looked down on,
now have a Big Man
on your side. Sad.

How Democracy Fails

If democracy fails blame democracy:
our belief that everyone is equal
and nobody is better than anyone
means we are unable to judge
the most able among us, qualified
to be leaders, make wise decisions

on behalf of our communities
and country. Without any standards
of rejection, we can go on being
who we say we are and never face
the fact that we are not who
we pretend to be.

        Whatever our problems,
Trump promises to fix them as
only he can. In spite of the blatant
failures of an administration
he asserts was the greatest
in history (has he ever read
a history book?), his followers,
in their blissful amnesia, accept
his not even remotely accurate
claims as true. And who are we
to doubt them? Why is one
opinion better than any other?

Part III

Leaving Valin

Al Suelo

My evening tapa hops begin at Bodega
Torre del Oro, where I first taste *gambas
al ajillo, pollo al ajillo, merluza en adobo,
pulpo en su tinta.* When I fold shucked
shrimp skins, olive pits, in my napkin,
"Al suelo!" the bartender scolds, brushing
my gathering to the sawdust-covered floor
for his aged assistant to sweep up later.

He slaps my glass and change on
the counter as if in anger, then I realize
it is a need to put rhythm in his work.
A guy on the stool next to mine says
the trouble with democracy is that you
can't get any hard-core movies, only
soft core. He thought after the death
of Franco he would be free to see it all.

Some tapa bars, concealed from tourists,
hide behind doors that look like any other.
At La Carbonería, once a high-ceilinged,
stone-walled cave where coal was stored,
a lively singles crowd fills the long tables
in several rooms, some nights feature
gypsy singers and flamenco dancers.

I live with Santos, a *sevillano* cabdriver,
and his California wife Barbara. He knows
bars on the shady side of Seville. Once
a professional thief asks for my shoe size.
Everyone smokes, when a woman holds
out a cigarette and asks, "Tienes fuego?"
I shake my head, she replies with
a sly smile, "Y follas?" (do you fuck?)

In Maro I enter my favorite bar
El Guapo through a glass-bead curtain.
The handsome owner complains
that no woman will sleep with him,
while a midget on a tall stool boasts
about the size of his cock. When I ask
for *horchata* (almond-milk), he brings
a *garnacha* (a liqueur). "For a moment,"
he says, "I thought you'd changed your life."

One evening the men gather at the bar
to watch on TV big-limbed Americans
in clown costumes do backflips, belly flops,
and walk-on-air tricks off the high board.
Even before the first one hits the water
with a prodigious splash, they shout
in astonishment, raising such a racket
the screen topples to the floor from its perch
on the shiny new expresso maker.

Chico a Chica

Discretely spaced along
the riverbank, couples
actively embrace inside
bulky unbuttoned coats.

I note their similar positions,
matched dark heads, imagine
they are whispering the same
tender words to each other.

The chico-a-chica ambiance
of Seville is always on display
along the Guadalquivir
beneath the Torre del Oro.

When I call her apartment
and ask for Carmen, who has
a novio, her mother says,
"Está en la calle."

A Street Named Serpents

The crippled woman on Sierpes
sells chances on the child.
"Niño, Niño," she cries,
the blind man, lottery tickets
pinned to his sleeve, taps his stick
on the stones and does not speak.
An old soldier, still in uniform,
props his crutches against
the stone wall to piss.

In Seville I see a surprising
number of cripples, everywhere
I look someone is missing
an arm or a leg or walks with
a club foot. Many stand on corners
calling out "para hoy" to sell
lottery tickets. It seems
the Franco regime passed a law
making handicapped people earn
a bare living in the street.

Galicia

Under the gray skies and green lands
of rainy Galicia, a hardy woman
in black leads an ox and cart
up a dirt road to a house of granite.

Some carrying buckets of shellfish
on their heads smile and seem happy.
Others kneel by the river
washing clothes on the rocks.

A girl in a bright dress balances
a jug on her head and swings
her hips on her way to the well
in the hope some male will notice.

A boy on a bicycle passes a man
on a burro and is overtaken in turn
by a motorbike then a Fiat speeds
down the middle of the road.

How did the bones of St. James
get from Cartagena to Galicia and
how did the church fathers authenticate
them eight-hundred years later?

A staff, gourd, hooded cape, a wide-
brimmed hat covered with cockleshells,
heavy-duty sandals, is what pilgrims wore
hiking to Santiago de Compostela.

In Asturias

At the local bar a man cuts
my hair for free as a woman pours
sparkling cider from a bottle
she holds above her head
into a wide-mouthed glass
positioned below her waist
to *escanciar* the drink—

this is called friendship,
these are neighbors, they like
each other and welcome
strangers. Here we find
a small pocket of people,
call them human beings,
who care about such things.

La Cueva de la Pileta

The chica snickers
placing one sure finger
on the phallic stalagmite
thrust up from the floor
of the cave, laughs
putting her hand
in the cold pond
seeking pesetas.

On the arched wall
behind her, pictures
painted in ochre
many millennia ago
of bulls and horses,
potent goats, men
with arms feathered
like eagles,

     but in
this Neolithic cave
superior to cathedrals
her eyes are set
on wet coins and mine
on what shifts,
like magic, beneath
her clinging blouse.

Saint Sebastian

Saint Sebastian might as well
be pairing his fingernails for all
the pain he shows as arrows turn
his skin into a pin cushion.

I remember how Jamie and I
in a Spanish art museum, not
the Prado, burst out laughing
after viewing several paintings

of Saint Sebastian displaying
his insouciant indifference
to repeated perforations.
How can we know a fish

is weeping? How can we
believe in Sebastian's wounds
if he doesn't give a fig to
show his exquisite agony?

Mirrors

Mirrors are windows
into a room you will
never enter, the Other
stares back with almost
your face but for
the grimace and hair
parted on the wrong side,
and the cold touch
of glass to a kiss
never refused,
never returned.

Pilar and her mother,
who has Alzheimer's,
enter an elevator
walled with mirrors
and her mother begins
talking to the woman
beside her. Later,
back in the elevator,
her mother says, "Look,
there are those two
women again."

Leaving Valin

Charming city by the Danube,
a large pedestrian-only area
in the town center, an extensive
tree-lined park along the river

to the fortress. We pass through
an industrial area mostly consisting
of abandoned Soviet-style factories,
a drab, depressing sight. Barbed-wire-

enclosed poured-concrete structures,
asbestos roofs, broken windows,
smoke-blackened walls, rusted
machine parts, scrap iron in the yard,

stripped pipes connecting nothing,
all a grim reminder of Eastern
Europe's failure to adapt, after
the Berlin Wall fell, to capitalist

competition. Workers left jobless
forced to fend for themselves,
some did, many didn't.
In their case, changes for the better

brought worse consequences.
Two or three factories restored,
new products for a new age,
the rest the detritus of history.

A Croatian Story

Serbian soldiers waving guns
come to her school, tell all
the students they have thirty
minutes to collect whatever
fits in a backpack and board
the waiting buses. A few try
to smuggle a beloved kitten
or puppy but soldiers seize
and shoot them on the road
in front of the bus—blood
spreads everywhere. She will
not see her home again until
turning fourteen, the house
in ruins, no roof or windows,
wet floors, the walls covered
with green mold.   She is angry
at her mother for leaving her,
not understanding how wars take
away free choice, she couldn't stay.
Like all Croatian men, her father
is off fighting, does not return—
shell-shocked, limbs intact—
until the war ends. He restores
the house and outbuildings,
now runs a prosperous farm.

Her husband works all day
disabling land mines, fears he
will be sent to Ukraine to do
the same dangerous work. She
tells her story as we sit at a long
table sampling local liquors
and pastries because she wants
the world to know how hard
it was for a very young girl
when Serbia invaded Croatia.

On the Rhine

The way to the castle
is steep, three switchbacks
the length of the ship.

Me, my pins are shot,
Achilles ready to snap,
bum plumbing.

In those days castle walls
were seven-feet thick,
people slept in beds

barely five-feet long.
For fear of death no one
slept on their back,

like a body in a coffin,
lest the Devil
snatch them away.

Shaw in Russia

George Bernard Shaw keeps Stalin's
portrait on the mantel by his bed.
On a tour of the Soviet Union
he throws food out the window
as the train is about to cross
the border into Ukraine (where millions
are starving) since he is sure
there are no shortages
under communist rule.

                        Shaw believes
that Russian prisoners are so happy
they are reluctant to leave,
a stay in prison a privilege superior
to working as a wage slave in Europe.
When he visits a collective farm
he is delighted to see the peasants
reciting his plays and singing songs
in praise of his work. Once he leaves,
these Potemkin peasants return
to their acting jobs in Moscow.

Shaw states that the West can not
afford to give itself moral airs just
because the Soviet Union, their most
enterprising neighbor, "humanely
and judiciously liquidates a handful
of exploiters and speculators to make
the world safe for honest men"—
After all, Stalin's five-year plans
move mountains, deliver the goods.

Fez

The medina at Fez
dates back more
than a millennium,
sharp odors from

the medieval tannery
truly smell that old
yet the exquisite
hand-tooled leatherwork

is ultrafashionable.
Streets so narrow
only donkeys
make deliveries.

Never enter unless
you remember
the way out
is the way in.

Barbados

Children rush the driver's side,
pantomime smoking and inhaling,
cry out "White man, white man,
Ganja, Ganja." Bare-chested boys
offer to wash or watch your car,
others settle for watching you.

At shacks and stalls of the market
barbecued fish and chicken,
jerked pork, curried goat, great
piles of fresh fruit for sale if you
don't mind the flies.

               The streets
are replete with opportunities
to break the seventh commandment
(a sign promises "Sexy Bad Girls")
or purchase controlled substances
for a modest fee. This is the land
of too much of a good thing.

Cuban Story

in memory of Amelia Hernández

One day in Havana ten students
ask to take a test early,
as they fill in the answers
she notices a cheat sheet under
an exam book, reports it,
and is told, "The revolution
needs those students."

As she leaves, a friend says,
"It's dark. I'd better walk you
to your car." At home her father
has received threatening calls.
He is angry with her for being
so brave. Students planted
in class ask provocative questions
to expose a teacher's sympathies.

"Is the standard of living higher
in Soviet Union or United States?"
She replies everybody knows
it's higher in the United States,
hears footsteps down the hall.
Realizing her mistake, she
slips out a side door,
runs to the U. S. embassy.

Part IV

The Starlings of Rome

The Starlings of Rome

At setting sun hundreds of thousands
swoop and swarm over the Vatican
and other vital organs of the city.
They mass together in ever-
changing formations, now compact,
now dispersed, rising and falling
until the last twilight before they
perch to do desecrating damage.

Since they feast by day on olive trees
viscous droppings spread and stick
to all surfaces, painting a vast canvas
of black and white Jackson Pollock
might envy. Romans find their
sunset murmurations in the sky
haunting, yet would prefer to do
without scraping up the mess.

Starlings from all parts of Europe
have been congregating in Rome
for more than a century. They feed
in the farmlands and by some telepathic
mystery agree to settle in the city
before dark. Their swirling designs
are synchronized as if a maestro
conducted their airborne symphony.

Why do they stir up such a dense
brew in the sky? For protection
it would seem. Their main enemy
are falcons who attack swiftly
with deadly force, but when
the starlings are all clumped
together in constant movement
a falcon can't lock in one target.

Is there a solution? Workers in
white protective smocks deploy
to vulnerable places with bullhorns
that screech out the calls of starlings
in distress. This eerie noise echoes
off nearby buildings and compels
the birds to seek better places to roost,
take their spattering to the suburbs.

The Rats of New York

for Joseph Mitchell

During World War II rat populations
in seaports soar, docks swarm with
scurrying rodents intent on sinking
sharp teeth into all sorts of cargo.

Rats nest in basements, feed off trash
in alleys, those from foreign lands
bring infections, even plagues,
despite fumigating ships from abroad.

Waterfront tenements, slaughterhouses,
outdoor markets draw more than their share,
the finest restaurants are not immune
to rat droppings in the steak tartar.

Central Park in summer is a favorite
spot, in the cold months they migrate
to adjacent apartment buildings,
the more elderly the more vulnerable.

They roam at night, lurk in the shadows,
make a mad dash across the street.
People who work the wee hours
often see them just before dawn.

One look at a crazy rat, all teeth and claws,
can shock you for life. Drunken Irishmen
talk of "seeing the rat" as Civil War soldiers
of "going to see the elephant."

Rats feed, fight, fuck, breed litters
of up to twenty about five times a year.
At four months they will do their own
multiplying, live three to four years.

Rats eat garbage scraps, also
the glue in book bindings, insulation
off telephone wires, shoe leather,
a lead pipe, if you own a backyard

orchard, a small farm, or store fruit
in the cellar, they will take a bite
out of each apple, each pear, steal eggs
from every hen, kill your poultry.

If you must, call Pied Piper Exterminators,
yet savvy old rats will kick a trap until
it snaps, if not poisoned nibble
proffered bait, the only proven way

to rid old buildings of rats is burn
the place down, start from scratch,
use cement and steel instead of wood,
seal every possible means of access.

Sometimes rats beat you to the punch,
set a fire by snatching matchbooks,
gnaw on phosphorous until it ignites,
abandon, so to speak, the sinking ship.

Rats are the world's best argument for cats.

Snake in the Lake

On a day so hot snakes
come out, one slides rippleless
into the lake, leaving
a stunned frog sprinkled
with blood, still as death.

Among swaying reeds,
forked tongue flickering,
biding time until it
can retrieve what
has been spit out half-

swallowed on the grass.
When the mauled frog
hops on three legs
down the muddy bank
and with splayed effort

swims for the far shore
small fish nibble the cut
from his severed foot.
The snake doesn't see
that zig-zagging escape,

keeping its intent eyes
on me, the spoiler,
then flashing a scaly back
of small copper coins
sinks into the lake.

Nuku Hiva Bugs

Stinkbugs don't smell as bad
as breadfruit rotting in the sand.
But if one should happen to fly
into your mouth, its taste is sharp,
and you are obliged, regardless
of the company, to spit it out.

Centipedes, a foot long, venomous,
seek warmth in slippers or under pillows.
Giant stag beetles, longest flying insects
in the world, thrive in rotten logs, blunder
about after nightfall. If they hit your skin
they cling with their piercing four-inch
mandibles. Entangled in your hair, they stay

for some time, once attached it takes
a flaming match's encouragement
to make them let go and leave. Worst
of all the *nono* flies, most dangerous
island creatures, walk your face,
camp out on your eyelids, ride food
all the way to your mouth.

So small you can barely see them,
but their fierce stings cause serious
swelling, a swarm can kill. One
wannabe starlet on *Survival* wore
only her bikini to show off her bod,
ended up with permanent scars.
Hollywood did not call.

Sunlight

Plants feed on light,
steal the sun's energy,
invent green leaves,
bright flowers, bees
buzz by to visit,
spread the good word,
honey is sweet
in the comb, tastes
great on baked bread.
A peach is a wedge
of wet sunlight.

When plants die
they decay into peat,
sink into the earth.
Add millenniums,
they turn to coal
sustaining the fire
that heats the house,
the blast furnace
that anneals steel—
coal is sunlight re-
cycled eons ago.

How Owls Kill

The owl, with its large eyes,
strikes its prey in total darkness.
How? Its big ears catch

the least sound of a mouse
scurrying in grass, dives
face-first toward the prey,

at the last second reverses
its body and hits the victim
with deadly talons.

An owl's asymmetric ears
detect where any movement
comes from and home in on

its prey's location. That's why
an owl can snatch a mole out
of a tunnel, a mouse under snow.

Web of Deceit

A spider's web is simply
an extension of its body,
it can sense the least
vibration at the far edge

and know where and what
is out there. A spider doesn't
budge from its center seat
for any passing wind

or falling leaf, yet a prey
caught and struggling gets
instant attention. Some
smaller spiders know how

to steal from larger ones,
cutting the web in order
to snatch what they want
without being detected.

Some insects that prey
on spiders might create
a false vibration, drawing
the spider to its doom.

Forked Tongues

Aristotle thought a snake's
forked tongue doubled
the pleasure of food
yet there are no taste buds
in the tongues of snakes.

The purpose is to help
sort out the smells of
the world and where
they come from so
the snake will stay
on the right track.

A forked tongue is
a map and a menu.

Death in the Dunes

1

Desert dunes thrum
with vibrations.
Insects make enough
sound for a sand
scorpion to sense.

Eight slits in its feet
detect slight signs
that disclose the steps
of its passing prey.
The scorpion shifts

to attack mode,
rising up, pincers
open, its eight feet
circling to note
the prey's location,

then moves closer,
pinchers ready to
seize the insect
and deliver
the lethal sting.

2

A doodlebug uses surface waves
in the sand to aid in hunting.
It digs a conical hole and buries

its plump body while keeping
its big jaws open and waiting
for a chance to trap the prey

in a carefully prepared pit.
If an ant falls in, the doodlebug
injects venom and that's that.

Elephants Have Long Noses

you must have noticed, smell
rules their world. The trunk
in constant motion to catch
each whiff. If you're in
the vicinity they will know
you by your smell from
any other human. If they
sense danger, up goes

a trunk and they run away
to hide in the tallest grass
they can find. Reunited
after a separation they flap
their ears, piss and shit
in great quantities, filling
the air with familiar scents.
Males can tell, through smell,
females are ready to mate

and of course distinguish
one gal in heat from another.
Because each elephant
is identified by its pee
they sense who's in
the herd or intruding
on their territory. They
even smell distant rain,
know when to mosey on.

Good (and Bad) Vibrations

Cats can feel vibrations
in their bellies, that's why
they crouch during a stalk
in order to know exactly

the location of their prey.
This is not the behavior
of a lazy lion, but of
big cats ready for the kill.

Once the earth shook
with the feet of huge
mammals bigger than
large elephants today,

and our ancestors walked
with bare feet on the earth
to sense the vibrations
that sang and spoke to them.

Bats

Birds hunt bugs by day,
bats work the night shift.
Their sonar system keeps
them from colliding with
stalactites in a dark cave.
The echoes of their calls
tell them how to navigate

the night air. This same
system helps them locate
and kill various insects.
When bats cry out we
do not hear them, their
high-decibel shrieks
sound like silence.

Losing It

If a squid loses the tip
of an arm to a rival squid
it knows it's been hurt,
its whole body reacts,
becomes hypersensitive,
but it doesn't know
which part suffered
the painful loss.

If a squid loses an arm
to a rival or a crab's pinchers,
it jets away squirting black ink.
The squid never touches
the severed spot, rather acts
as if its whole body
was one big sore.

Unlike a squid,
an octopus knows if
one of its arms
has lost a tip, or been
otherwise injured.
The wounded limb
is cradled to protect it
from further harm.

A Zebra's Stripes

You probably think
a zebra's stripes
serve as camouflage,
yet their main predators
hunt by night, a lion's
eyes are not sharp enough
to see stripes in the dark,
they see a gray donkey
or horse of some sort.

The real reason zebras
have stripes is to confuse
bloodsucking fleas who
for some strange reason
bungle their landings
on the striped beast
and aren't able to drink
a full quota of blood.

The Choice

A squirrel clinging
to a tree outside
the library, a hawk
on the limb above.
Each time the hawk

switches limbs
the squirrel
switches sides
of the trunk. Snow
covers the ground.

The nearest tree is
far away. Should I
frighten the hawk?
It would only
come back. And if

I step closer
the squirrel might
make a break for it
and the hawk would
swoop in for the kill.

So I walk home,
leaving the squirrel
still clinging to the tree.
the hawk perched
on the limb above.

On Leeches

If you fall into muddy river water
and feel leeches feeding on your legs
the best advice is not to pull them
off and leave their jaws in your flesh

or to apply a cigarette to burn them
only to see a splatter of blood,
rather let them finish their meal
in peace, exit on their own accord—

less harm done all around—at least
that's what the doctor tells me.
Remember, leeches once were agents
of healing, their saliva is beneficial,

but too much of this good thing
can prove fatal by taking an excess
of your precious blood—just ask
the late George Washington.

Part V

Trying to Say

Alms for Oblivion

Some suicides kill
not only themselves
but also their identity,
traveling to a remote
place, getting rid
of clothes, rings,
wallets, whatever,
so that the body—
if anything is found
besides a skeleton
that can't be traced—
is nameless. Instead
of heaven or hell,
some of the dead
choose oblivion.

Perhaps the best way
to be resurrected
is to be forgotten.
Sometimes oblivion
is the gateway to
great fame. Consider
the case of Tutankhamen.
Or better yet the cave
paintings of Lascaux,
unknown for more than
twenty thousand years
the walls are still alive
with spear-bearing men
hunting horned animals.

Boccaccio's Theft

In the Dark Ages as only rats
digest the classics and the light
of learning is a guttering candle,
Boccaccio visits the Benedictine
Abbey in Monte Casino, finds
the library in a deplorable state:
the door unbolted, left open,

grass spouting on windowsills,
manuscripts coated with dust,
torn pages scattered on the floor,
precious parchments mutilated,
ripped into strips to make psalters
for boys, amulets for women,
sold for a few *soldi.* Reduced

to tears, or so he says, he leaves
the desolate place in despair,
but not before he retrieves
from that scene of neglect
the sole surviving manuscripts
of Books 11-16 of the *Annals,*
what remains of the *Histories*

by one Cornelius Tacitus
as well as works by Varro
and Apuleius, including
The Golden Ass. The question
is: Did Boccaccio tell a tall
tale to cover up his theft?

Either way, we say thanks.

The Myth of Flight

for Hugh Kenner

The classical assumption is
sons should obey fathers,
but had he not built the device
to satisfy the queen's lust
and the labyrinth to contain her
monstrous get, what need
to invent the wings of wax
tempting the boy to soar
too high, lose his feathers
to the relentless sun, fall
to a watery death?

The strange marriage on
a sandflat of a box kite
and a bicycle, the damn
contraption achieving flight,
what happened at Kitty Hawk
is in all the books, but what
the Wright boys did is as much
part myth as what a designing
father once made to free
his son from an amazed
Minotaur's dominion.

Masters Class

"I have a horror of a white sheet of paper."
　　　　　　　　　—Redon

The Great American Masters
wrote books about
writing the book:
Hester is the muse
and Pearl the wild work
out of control.

You need an integration
of black and white
to write—
the words drain
from the vein,
blot, clot
on the page.
What is said
must be bled:
The Scarlet Letter.

And Huck and Jim
trying to ride
that wide river
of language.

And Melville,
trying to say,
thrusts his pen
like a harpoon
at the page,
until Ishmael, mad Ahab,

and Queequeg,
dark as ink,
meet their apotheosis—
the whale breeches,
a great salt reproach,
white as a sheet!

On Poetry

A *plastique,* e. e. cummings says,
is easier than poetry, a great poem
keeps detonating as long as readers
have ears to hear. To begin: take
a deep breath then release words
by the lungful as the heart beats
against the stress; say it straight
and get out, leaving clear images
and a clarity of thought.
      Poetry
is simply and only those times
when language yields imperishable
eloquence, the unfading flavor
of choice words tasting perfect
in the mouth, the loving syllables
rubbing together in sonorous bliss,
the frenzied world finding a brief,
bright, particular focus.
      True poets
ask all those wallflower words
to rise up and dance; perhaps,
as Flaubert lamented, a tune
banged out on a cracked pot
to set a bear to bopping, when
we strive to make the stars
weep for our melodies.

                    As long as
there's life in it, as long as poets
love their words well, take
pains to present their best
acts of attention, then poetry
can still give us the pleasure
to experience the incongruous
truths of the world.
                    I'm talking
about genuine wordslingers taking
command of our common tongue.

Just Beat It

I saw the best minds of my generation
fuck themselves up big time,
Ginsberg declares, meaning he
and his buddies take too many mind-
altering drugs. Poetry is written
in reverie, revised with lucidity,
the Beats skip the second part.

They see themselves as hipsters
blowing riffs on an unspooling roll
of paper (I see another analogy),
giving poetry-as-jazz readings
in coffeehouse cellars, everybody
dresses in black, wears shades,
but it seems nobody gives a damn
about how messy words can be
on the page. We want our poets
to act out the life of the poet,

the more outrageous the more
self-destructive the more authentic
is the going notion. Poets should
flame out at an early age, drunken
staggers, maniacal rages, hooked on
those ironically named controlled
substances, bipolar, bisexual, gender-
bending lifestyles the preferred
modus operandi. What I fart is art
might as well be the motto, an in-
comprehensible sprawl on the page
proof of a bearded bard's genius.

Trying to Say

things happen we
talk about them
      not that
the telling comes up
to the event
      not that
speech equals deed
      still
the telling will continue
elaborating with
inadequate words
      not that
it does any good
      not that
saying explains doing
      not that
words and the world
are the same
      not that
we'll ever stop

The Death of Lorca

for Ian Gibson

He dislikes Protestant churches,
big organ instead of high altar,
minister's sermon in Spanish
facing the congregation; the priest,
back to the laity, speaks in Latin.

Shoes that do not move remind
him of death, all the dead bodies
he sees as a boy are laid out flat
on their backs, dressed in their
Sunday best, wearing shoes.

He is friends with Salvador Dalí,
Luis Buñuel, and other great
creators of his generation, plays
a key role in a Spanish renaissance
of poetry, drama, art, and film.

Yet in his hometown of Granada
he is "The Fag with the Bow Tie."
As Civil War spreads across
Andalusia he refuses to escape
to the Republican side for fear of
being trapped in a no-man's zone.

Lorca is arrested. General Queipo
De Llano, the Butcher of Seville,
tells the commandant at Granada
to give the poet, "coffee,
plenty of coffee."

The Black Squad takes him
to the nearby resort town of Viznar,
favorite site to execute loyalists.
(one witness cries out, "Murderers!
You're going to kill a genius!")

Told he will be shot, Lorca asks
for a last confession, but the priest
is gone. Before dawn he is shoved
in a truck with two bullfighters
and a teacher with a wooden leg.

They are killed at Fuente Grande,
a famous spring known in Arab times
as "the Fountain of Terror." Later,
one murderer boasts, "Two bullets
in the ass for being queer."

Purple Birds

Masterpieces are hard,
manifestos, conversation
pieces are easy. Here's
a woman who does sculptures
of babies popping out of
toasters, the whole thing
drenched in a blend of
blue-and-yellow paints—
her statement.

And here's
a artist who paints weird
purple birds distinctively;
he's good with his brushes,
we recognize his paintings,
but who *needs* purple birds?
What purpose do they serve?

I know we're not supposed
to ask these questions—

instead critics will praise
the artist's unique subject
and style and people will
buy her toasters, his paintings,
prominently display them
on their sideboard or wall
(they're fun to talk about),
wait for the price to rise.

Artists: Then & Now

Are those broken pots
archeologists find in middens
due to slippery fingers,
floors of stone, or is it that
some finicky pot-thrower
seeking perfection
in a cup, a bowl, a plate,
smashes in frustration
askew efforts that fail
to meet her standards,
achieve a work of art,
just as a writer, in the days
of typewriters, pulls out
a botched sheet, crumples it,
sends it sailing toward
a circular file overflowing
in a far corner of the room.

The New Wave

(La Nouvelle Vague)

A drunken man in a white suit
walks with a cane on the beach,
dead gull in the sand, Jean
Seberg's face, a razor blade
taken out and replaced, cliffs,
gulls circle in the sky,
shirts buttoned and unbuttoned,
Jean Seberg's face, snug in
a fuzzy white bathrobe she
hugs herself, sun on the sand,
a man with a cane, Jean
Seberg's face, hair
concentration-camp short,
dead bird in the sand.

An unshaven man spits
on a glass door, drops some
cash on the floor, a long
dialogue about angst, ennui,
two shots are fired, Jean
Seberg's face, a lone tear
in the corner of an eye, a gun
is pointed, a drunken man
waves his cane, speculates
about how much jockeys weigh,
a lawman, chewing a stick
of gum, hits Jean's fiancé
on the head with his pistol.

Jean walks arm-in-arm
with her beau on the beach,
the policeman takes aim at
the man in the white coat,
a boy, shirt unbuttoned
to the waist, stabs the officer,

still chewing gum, in the back,
Jean Seberg in a white dress
walks the beach alone, her guy
is gone, the wind is blowing,
two men follow her, the boy
runs into the raging surf, Jean
Seberg's face in a slow fade.

John Wayne Stars as Sarge

Pinned down on the beach
Sarge smokes while
the hot heads get shot up.
When the skipper gives
the word to move out
Sarge leads the way,
the extras waddle after.

These American killers
are twelve inches high
in black and white
and have metal heads.
Each has a gun and a shit-
eating grin breaks through
the grime whenever
another Jap bites dust.

After the island is secured
and Old Glory flaps over
the long chow line, the boys
on leave will get laid by
grateful girls in Hawaii.

But Sarge stays behind
dreaming of another beachhead
and the next batch
of green recruits, laughing
to himself as they unload
their gear, "They're getting
younger every time."

Count Dracula

There's blood on the bell rope,
a body swinging upside down
by the heels like a clapper,
a trip to the fog-shrouded
cemetery spices the mystery.
The count with bloody lips
has risen from the grave,
returned to his dread castle
on the cloud-covered pinnacle,
with widening eyes he compels
his victims to come to him.
Even the priest, secretly
in league with the minions
of evil, returns, his high
white collar hiding telltale
marks on his neck

Despite garlic and crucifix
the vampire, aided by a mighty
wind shattering the window,
enters the bedroom and stands,
a black-caped tower of strength,
before a woman in a negligee,
who willing against her will
unbuttons her bodice and lifts
her face for his strange kiss.

The big-jawed boyfriend
is no match for the elegant
man of evil who smacks
him down and takes his girl
back to the castle where she
wears low-cut gowns,
a choker at her throat,
secretly visits the cellar to
embrace the count's coffin.

The cowardly townspeople
live on in the vain hope that
if they leave the count alone
he won't molest their women,
despite the loss of various
lovely daughters on nights
when under a full moon
wolves howl in the forest.

It takes a stake shaped
like a giant pencil to stab
the pointy toothed beast
in the heart. At the end
the hero looks down on
the bloody-eyed corpse
of the evil count, makes
the sign of the cross, then
rides off to copulate with
his baffled bride to be
who sometimes awakes
in the dead of the night,
softly touches her neck.

Part VI

Waiting for the End

Waiting for the End

It's like Pompeii, Vesuvius
has erupted and the lava
is headed our way, this time
in particles and droplets
slowly, yet far too fast; around
the world people are dying
in appalling numbers, often
but not exclusively among
old folk like me.

      If reports can be
believed, all this because
a vendor in a Wuhan, China,
food market caught the virus
from an infected bat (or
a leak from a nearby lab?),
starting a pandemic so infectious
people catch it by touching
their face and, for several
lethal months, no vaccine.

During those direful days
I reread Camus, since this
surely is an existential crisis,
our all-too-human lives occur
within incongruous contexts
of absurdity. Like Sisyphus
we roll a rock up a hill then
it rolls back down again,
yet dignity is in the effort,
even a kind of happiness.

Brave healthcare workers
become our secular saints,
an unventilated circle in hell
reserved for inept leaders.
Only we can give meaning
to life, our spirit sustains
the best that is in us. We
also can be the cause of
unspeakable evil. For now
I ask only mercy on us all—
Those who shall live or die.

Night Nurse

Twelve-hour shifts in the ICU
watching Covid-19 patients take
their last dwindling breaths,
unmasked people standing vigil
outside the hospital insist
their relatives on ventilators
only have the flu. If the hospital
claims otherwise, it's to grab
more federal dollars.

                Local preachers
praise a God stronger than
any virus since true believers
who pray to Him will never die.
Those she inoculates say
the syringe is empty, she must be
getting kickbacks from Pfizer
for peddling their fake vaccine.

She is a hero in a war many in
her town think isn't happening,
a hoax. At the grocery store
checkout counter they joke about
the fools who wear masks.
Don't take it serious, they say,
it's a Democrat plot, once
Biden's in office after the rigged
election it will all go away.

If someone comes off
the ventilator and survives,
people credit God, not doctors,
nurses, or treatments. It's a miracle,
not modern medicine, that saves them.

When one of her patients dies,
she weeps until her ribs ache.

Posthumous Poems

Sometimes I feel like I'm living
a posthumous life, Covid kills
a million of us as well as a part
of everyone who survives.

It deadens our hearts to save us
from too much mourning,
from placing exclusive blame
on Donald and his Gargoyles

for inoculating us against good
advice, necessary precautions.
We know now that about half
who died didn't get vaccinated

at all or often enough, others
had pre-existing conditions
but then don't we all have
pre-existing conditions?

I might call this collection
Posthumous Poems, even though
at the moment I'm still alive,
though sometimes I feel like

a disembodied spirit invisibly
watching life go on as if existence
makes sense, means something,
is going someplace other than
the black hole of oblivion.

The Scan

The surgeon's assistant doctor,
straight out of med school,
has a bedside manner that puts
my teeth on edge. He talks
like a trip hammer and his heart,
I'd guess, is made from one of
the harder stones. "Do you feel
any pain?" he asks as strong

fingers probe my stomach.
"A little," I say after one
vicelike squeeze. "I felt something,"
he announces and orders
a CAT scan, adding in passing,
"It might have been food."
I spend several anxious nights
prior to the exam—the usual

fear of dying before my time,
before my work is done.
The guy who preps me
is even younger and chews
gum incessantly as he tries,
unsuccessfully, to wed needle
and vein. "Two's my limit,"
he says, shaking his head,

snap-snapping his gum.
The woman monitoring
the machine gives it a try.
"Shit, it blew," she cries out,
succeeds on the second jab.
The scan, by the way,
is clean and for now
I'm sleeping soundly.

Blue Water House

1

My hands grip her shoulders
as Roser leads me across the hot
sand dunes of the Delaware Bay.
The beach has gentle waves,
unlike the riptides of the Atlantic
a few miles away. We watch
the ferry bound for Cape May
sail off to return later, only
without sails, just a white ship
shrinking and then fading
from sight over the horizon.

2

I need Roser's support again
to wade across the sliding sands,
seaweed, and pebbles on the shore.
When the water is waist-high
I swim a few strokes, or, better yet,
lie on my back and float, eyes shut
against the burning sun. Pounds
I've gained lately come in handy,
a mere flutter of my hands keeps
my belly above water, so restful
if I fell asleep I'd only drift back
to shore and awake at the soft
touch of sand and smooth pebbles.

3

Lewes, Delaware, is a summer secret
kept by a happy few. Our favorite place
is the Blue Water House, a short walk
to the beach. We stay in the Hemingway
Suite, a mini-museum displaying
photos of Papa, a desk featuring

an Underwood with its clickity-
clack keys and carriage return.
The main motif is African safari:
plaster heads of zebras, lions,
elephants line the walls, our bed
is of polished logs with leopard-
skin-patterned sheets. On the ceiling
are paddles, a tiger hide, assorted hats,
but, thankfully, no hunting rifles.

Jimmy Buffet

My thanks to Jimmy Buffet,
who died the other day,
for those salt-rimmed drinks

I savor at Margaritaville;
put the blame on him for
middle-aged men that sport

beer bellies, dress as slovenly
as the weather will allow:
baggy Bermudas barely

held up by a shrinking butt,
flip-flops and a T-shirt
sagging at the neck above

stains of pizzas past and
a logo on the front with its
Dean Martin wisecrack:

I'd rather have a bottle
in front of me than
a frontal lobotomy.

Key West Redux

In our posthumous post-Covid life
we find ourselves back in Key West,
a treasured place we thought we might
never see again. At the Hibiscus Motel

swimming pool a group of American
Midwesterners stand armpit deep
in blue water, beer cans sitting
on the pool's ledge. They talk and talk

and never swim. Several bald men
make no effort to protect their skulls
from the fierce rays of the sun.
In keeping with the national average,

they are all overweight. One man
asks some nearby laughing women,
each with a pink drink in a plastic glass,
"What are you celebrating, ladies?"

The reply, "Not being in Indiana."

Nobody's Home

The lights are on
but nobody's home,
I've known people

like that, remote
when alone or even
when among friends,

they remind me of
an empty dock whose
ship is lost at sea.

On Memory and Forgetting

1

Memory is a second chance
to set the record straight
or crooked, as you will,
recall a past that never was

thus making a better story
that doesn't reflect discredit
on you, cleans up the blood,
so to speak, wipes away

incriminating fingerprints,
heals old wounds—if that
is possible. It's not nostalgia,
exactly, yet it paints clearer

pictures for good or ill. It can
be an apology, an opportunity
to place blame where it may
not belong, to make amends.

2

Forgetting is the best
form of forgiveness,
memory and revenge
go together no matter
how cold the dish.

I've heard we dream
in order to forget
otherwise the brain
would clutter up like
a sprawling landfill.

Soldiers home from
war wish they didn't
remember—if only
they could blot out
the horrific scenes.

Call me Lethe,
I forget just why.

The Ancients

Unlike us, moping around
in fear of death, the Ancients
in both hemispheres did something
about it, or rather if you are
número uno you have your people
do something about it like piling
up stone on stone for years to build
monuments of prodigious height
to hold your body, skin and bones,
your innards discretely set
aside in an urn.

What's the idea behind
these huge heaps of stones?
Some might say they serve as
a large marker for extraterrestrials
to zoom to the rescue, others
that they're meant to intimidate
tomb robbers from filching

all your stuff, but my hunch is
it is to display your power
in this our life, making all those
lesser people do your whimsical
bidding, for a time, as long as
you are *número uno*.

The Invention of Love

When couples first copulated
face to face a new era began.
Love walked in the front door,
what your mate looked like
suddenly mattered, even more
how he or she looked
at you, what eye contact
and wide smiles meant.

Touching front to front,
skin on skin, was exquisite,
the just-right warmth of it,
those kisses that mark
the invention of love
as a soulful delight,
the selection of the fittest,
Darwin called it, meaning
how much life depends on
finding the best match.

Ghosts

1

You have to admit the dead
are reluctant to talk,
yet we want them
to communicate so badly
we claim to hear voices,
see them in our sleep,
lurking in the penumbra
of a shadow we glimpse
a fleeting outline, not
enough to swear by,
or put any faith in,
but we do anyway,
that's how needy
we are of ghosts,
why we refuse to ever
let them leave.

2

The fleshless dead
come back to us
as ghosts, a presence
felt but seldom seen,
vaguely a fleeting
image in the mind.
We see faces most
clearly in dreams,
eyes probe into us
but lips are sealed.
We never know if
they want to talk,
offer advice, send
love, or, what we
fear most: a curse.

The Digital Age

How did fingers become
so sensitive? The simple
answer: picking fleas off
themselves and others,
thus was patience born,
a kind of delicacy. The art
of grooming our kin
is basic. In monkeys
the quest is usually not
for lice but flakes of skin
and other tiny particles.
Picking and scratching of
fur or hair give pleasure.

A man is known by how
firmly he shakes hands,
a display of personal power,
a prophecy of his longevity.
"Get a grip," we tell a person
metaphorically losing a grasp
on the important things,
sometimes literally their place
in the world. "Hang in there,"
we say, shorthand for urging
people to cling to what
remains of dear life.

Old Guy

1

In my forties I said
"I'm playing the back nine."
Now, clubhouse in sight,
my best hope is to double
bogey the eighteenth hole.

At a Barcelona restaurant
I hear two men switch
the metaphor to soccer.
"We're in discount time,"
one says, the other is
more dire: "We're in
final penalty kicks."

2

In the middle of the night
my metaphysical moment:
old guy, prostate, that story.
Shuffling my Frankenstein amble
down the hall I sit and piss
in dribs and drabs several times
each night as years slide away.
I'm not the first, nor the last.

This is the way the world goes
for all us old guys. Eyes dim,
knees shot, bum plumbing,
clogged pipes, my ticker
sometimes skips a tock.
A few hours of sleep,
then a few more, until one day
that last alarm rings.

Ode to Alzheimer's

One by one the words
slip away, the names
of people we knew,
places we treasured,
thoughts we once

could think are gone,
feelings we once felt
we could articulate
are no longer there.
Books we once knew

by heart now fade
as we turn the page.
One by one the words
slipping away; then,
one day, the world.

The Fall

We pay a price for
those distant ancestors
once having the audacity
to stand on their own two feet,
the law of gravity has it in
for our poor spinal cord,
disks slip, vertebrae feel
the wear and tear, arches
fall, hip and knee joints
grind to a halt.

It hasn't happened,
yet it will come.
Bum knees, shaky legs,
an unsteady balance,
one day I will topple
to the floor—with luck
a thick carpet, not wood,
hard tiles, or linoleum.

          Will I
break something is
the question: an arm,
a leg, worst of all
a hip or hit my head,
and if no one is
there to help me,
the plot takes a dark
turn. Even if nothing

happens and I am able
to rise up by myself,
the good news will
only last so long before
I take another tumble
and fall again. That
is the fate in store
for all us old folk,
sooner or later
we all fall down.

Thick Milkshakes

for Jim Vincent

Jim tells his dad that it looks like
he isn't going to last much longer
and asks if he has anything he
wants to say, any advice to pass on:
buy IBM stock, brush your teeth,
whatever. At first his dad shakes
his head, he has nothing special
to convey, but then he says,

"There is one thing—milkshakes.
I have never liked thick milkshakes
where the ice cream jams the straw;
here at the hospital they make
them thin, they go right up
the straw, that's the way they
were when I was a boy. I've never
liked thick milkshakes."

After his dad dies Jim's mother
admits that she wished he
had said something to her,
told her she'd been a good wife,
that he loved her, but he died
without saying anything like that.

I ask Jim if he said anything
to him. "He did," Jim answers,
"he told me he never liked
thick milkshakes."

Dad's Last Days

The Pope today is too ill
to say Merry Christmas in
so many languages, Jimmy
Stewart raises a weary arm
to cameramen on his return
to the hospital, I call Dad
to wish him happy birthday,
his wife says he still won't
wear a hat in the cold.

On his deathbed he tells me
to take good care of my wife,
in the end it's the only thing
a man has, but what son
can understand his father's
last words, who were close
too short, apart too long?

The final time I see my father,
half-naked, dressing gown askew,
half-conscious from medications
easing him out of life, I say,
"Goodbye, Dad" and touch
his bare big toe as I leave.

The Future

I've always been curious
about the centuries before
I was born, now I worry

about the years I will miss.
I must admit my mind
tells me that the world

at present is taking a turn
for the worse, as if things
weren't terrible enough

as they are. Temperatures
will climb, water will rise,
bad weather of all sorts

will wreak havoc across
our vulnerable globe.
China, smiling benignly

as if nothing were wrong,
will spread tendrils, taking
whatever its empire needs.

As for us, will we be up
to the task of defending
our identity or integrity?

Will the dumb keep
dumbing down, the smart
still outsmart themselves,

and whatever the case is,
however unacceptable,
will it be accepted?

A Note on the Poems

While all of these poems reflect my sensibility, not all are based on personal experience. In Part I, in several poems I try to dramatize experiences of my generation: "Remembering the Fifties," "Chicago, 1968," "Bringing the War Home," "Shut It Down," "At the Commune," "Jail, No Bail," and in Part III, while I have visited islands in the Caribbean, I have never been to Barbados. "How Owls Kill," "Web of Deceit," "Forked Tongues," "Death in the Dunes," "Elephants Have Long Ears," "Good (and Bad) Vibrations," "Bats," "Losing It," and "A Zebra's Stripes," were inspired by Ed Yong's *An Immense World: How Animal Senses Reveal the Hidden Realms Around Us.*

About the Author

William Heath was born in Youngstown, Ohio, on 27 June 1942. A graduate of Hiram College, with a Ph.D. in American Studies from Case Western Reserve, he has taught American literature and creative writing at Kenyon, Transylvania, Vassar, and the University of Seville as the Fulbright professor of American literature. Since 1981 he taught at Mount Saint Mary's University, where he edited *The Monocacy Valley Review,* which won national awards for excellence, and retired in 2007as a Professor Emeritus. The William Heath Award is given annually to honor a student writer. In 2008–9 he was the Sophia M. Libman Professor of Humanities at Hood College. In 2022 he received the Lifetime Achievement Award from Hiram.

Heath's novel about the civil rights movement in Mississippi, *The Children Bob Moses Led* (Milkweed Editions, 1995, paperback 1997), won the Hackney Literary Award for best novel, was nominated for the National Book Award and the Pulitzer Prize, and by Joyce Carol Oates for the Ainsfield-Wolf Award. *Time* magazine selected it as one of eleven outstanding novels on the African-American experience. A twentieth anniversary edition was published by NewSouth Books in 2014. His second novel, *Blacksnake's Path: The True Adventures of William Wells* (Heritage Books, 2008), was nominated for the James Fenimore Cooper Award and chosen by the History Book Club as an alternate selection. *Devil Dancer* (Somondoco Press, 2013) is a neo-noir crime novel set in Lexington, KY. *William Wells and the Struggle for the Old Northwest* (University of Oklahoma Press, 2015, paperback 2017) won two Spur Awards for best history book and best first nonfiction book and the Oliver Hazard Perry Award for military history. He also edited *Conversations with Robert Stone* (University of Mississippi Press 2016, paperback 2018). His forty book reviews and twenty essays on Hawthorne, Melville, Twain,

William Styron, Thomas Berger, Robert Stone, and Frank Bergon, among others, as well as historical studies of Thomas Morton and William Wells have appeared in various newspapers, scholarly journals, literary magazines, reviews, and anthologies.

Heath began publishing his poetry in the late sixties; the best are collected in *The Walking Man* (Icarus Books, 1994). James Wright said of this early work: "William Heath is in my opinion one of the most brilliantly accomplished and gifted young poets to appear in the United States in quite some time. I am especially moved by the delicacy and precision of the language, which indicates a distinguished intelligence, and by the purity and depth of feeling in all of his poems." Richard Wilbur noted: *"The Walking Man* is the work of a poet who knows how to tell a story."

Steel Valley Elegy (Kelsay Books, 2022), selects later work set in the U.S., including poems from a chapbook, *Night Moves in Ohio* (Finishing Line Press, 2019). Kit Hathaway noted that these poems "are by turns poignant, funny, and starkly realistic, teeming with fascinating storyline detail and imagery." Eamon Grennan added, "These poems are savvy and lively, as exact as a high jumper's focus, quick and accurate as a tennis player's eye, wrist, ankle . . . Heath's own remembrance of things past—an autobiography in rapt miniature lit by the laser-light of memory."

Going Places (Kelsay Books, 2023), set abroad, is the companion volume to *Steel Valley Elegy*. All the poems display an eye for telling detail, a lucid perspective, an ironic, witty, thoughtful sensibility, sonorous words, memorable narrative, a deft way of moving a poem down the page. As Esperanza Hope Snyder stated, "William Heath is a master of describing his journeys to exotic and challenging places in the world, where people, history, art, and natural beauty inspire his poetry. Few poets understand the fragility of the world as deeply as Heath does."

Alms for Oblivion (Kelsay Books, 2024) contains poems set at home and abroad, including autobiography, social commentary, travels, the natural world, the art of poetry, aging, and death.

Inventing the Americas (Finishing Line Press, 2024) is a chapbook of poems on Columbus and Vespucci in the Western Hemisphere.

He and his wife, Roser Caminals-Heath—author of ten novels in Catalan—lived in Frederick, MD since 1981 and moved to Annapolis in 2022.

Visit:
www.williamheathbooks.com

www.ingramcontent.com/pod-product-compliance
Lightning Source LLC
Chambersburg PA
CBHW022117160426
43197CB00009B/1061